Dear Black Girl

*Equip * Empower * Enlighten*

Kimberly Lowe Abad

Dedication

This book is dedicated to a few black women whom I adore. They are the reason I am who I am today, and for that, I am grateful.

Minnie Lawson Gordon – my beautiful mother. You are more than my mother, you are my friend. You were my first teacher and cheerleader. Because of you, I was able to dream – I mean dream big! You made me believe I could do anything I wanted to do and be anyone I wanted to be. You taught me how to be a lady and for that, I honor you. I am because you are. Thank you mama for everything. You are the wind beneath my wings. I love you.

Leslie Parrish Heard – mother dearest. You didn't give me life, but life gave me you. I will never understand why the Lord loved me so much to bless my life with you. Thank you for being the best thing I never knew I needed. I simply adore you.

Kristal Verneda Lowe Johnson – my sister and best friend. Your support and love for me has been overwhelmingly amazing. Thank you for everything. I love you more than you will ever know.

Anna Coley Lyons – my godmother in heaven. Lord knows I miss you every day. Thank you for praying for me. Your prayers are still carrying me. I can't wait to see you in heaven. Love is too weak to describe how I feel about you.

You four women are ocular demonstrations of black girl magic!

Last, but not least, my daughters Karis Rae and Kaius Raye. Everything I do, I do it for you two. You girls are truly living up to your names...Grace and Joy. Mommy loves you both to life.

Acknowledgements

Wow! I can't believe I did it! I really wrote a book!!! There are so many people I must thank.

First and foremost, thank you Jesus. I made You a vow years ago that you would get a return on your investment. I am humbled you chose me for such a task and time as this.

To the love of my life, the one God created just for me, my husband, Rashad. You are, in large part, why I was able to complete this project. Your encouragement has meant everything to me. There is no way I could have done this without your love and support. The way you have encouraged me throughout this entire process has been remarkable. The girls and I are beyond blessed to have you in our lives. My prayer is that God will continue to keep us on this journey. "What we have is much more than they can see..."

Karis Rae and Kaius Raye Abad, my precious angels on earth – God knew that I needed you two to complete this book. Although I have many "children," I needed to birth you two to truly understand the magnitude of this assignment. I pray God blesses me with health and life to raise you two. Mommy loves you both past the moon and stars.

To my family – my mama, my daddy, my sister, and brother, thank you for always believing in me and encouraging me in all of the endeavors that I have embarked on. I love you all more than you will ever know. And to my siblings, thank you, thank you, thank you! We know that Love Out Weighs Everything! (LOWE).

To my best friends on this side of heaven – LaKisha and Sharrita – I love y'all! Over 20 years of friendship has been incredible to share with you both. The way you gals support me is what every black girl should experience in this life. The wonderful memories we have shared made *Dear Black Girl* possible. You all are the definition of true, authentic, genuine friendship. I am beyond grateful.

To my forever friends Dawn and Candice – thank you for being who you are to me. I cherish the bond that we share. I love y'all to life and beyond.

To my Mark 2 friend Ashley Johnson – God knew I needed you. I will always need you. I just love me some you!

To the students who have allowed me to speak into their lives, listened to my rants, and allowed me to influence their way of thinking – thank you for trusting me. Believing that I had something that you needed/wanted to hear is humbling. You all are incredible.

To everyone else that sees me the way the Lord sees me – the goodness, the greatness, the phenomenal woman who I strive to be every day – much obliged! Thank you very, very much!!

My heart is full.

Kim

Table Of Contents

Introduction

In a world where we are still shouting "Black Lives Matter" it is important to create a safe space for the different sectors of the black race. Black girls are often viewed as loud, boisterous, confrontational and just plain mean. They are placed in boxes and are often times not given the space to allow their light to shine. But, before they can allow their lights to shine, they first have to know that they have a light within. Other people and races are threatened by this inside light that the black girl carries, so sometimes, it is dimmed even before it can be discovered. The idea that a black girl could change the world frightens a lot of demographics and as a result, some black girls never reach their full potential. Unknown self-hate and not being properly nurtured also add to the demise of the light that black girls have in them. As an educator for over a decade, I have encountered several black girls who are afraid to do the work to become who they are destined to be. Others simply do not know how or where to start. As a result, they settle for mediocrity and what seems to be "safe."

By no stretch of the imagination is this *Dear Black Girl* "the gospel." It is merely a guide to offer black girls a different perspective and to add to what they already know. I also hope to shed some light on that which is unknown and tap into untapped inner thoughts. It is my desire that every black girl who reads this book finds something valuable that can be taken away or tucked inside. I hope to plant seeds and allow life to water those seeds. And when those seeds are ready to bloom, she will blossom in full force...becoming the beautiful, amazing, strong, intelligent black girl she was created to be.

Dear Black Girl is designed to be interactive. After every chapter, an opportunity for reflection will be provided. It is my desire that reflections will occur for the purpose of enhancement and growth. I believe in black women. I trust black women. I love black women. I am a black woman.

Keeping It Real

Dear Black Girl,

This phrase has been coined to denote when someone is telling the honest truth about something. Over the years, this phrase has come to have a negative stigma attached to it. When a black girl declares she's about to "keep it real" that usually mean she is about to give someone a piece of her mind. Beautiful black girl, I am going to keep it real and explain some things to you. This book is designed to help you and make you think and reflect. It will offer a different perspective, uplift, include, and build up the black girl. *Dear Black Girl* is also designed to be interactive, allowing time for reflection and consideration. I am excited about what you will read in the chapters to come. Please take time to understand my heart in the next few pages. I am here for you, black girl. Thank you for allowing me the keep it real!

Reflection

What do you hope to gain from reading this book?

_____

_____

_____

_____

_____

Love Yourself

Dear Black Girl,

Love is not a feeling, it's a choice. Feelings change over time. Think of the things you loved as a little girl – your favorite toy or that bicycle that you received for Christmas. Think about how you "feel" about it now. I mean, you may not hate it, but you don't love it like you did as a child. When dealing with yourself, you first have to choose to love you – flaws and all. Once you make the choice to love you, commit to making good choices to love you even the more. In taking care of yourself, understand that you don't have to tear yourself in pieces to keep others whole. Don't stretch yourself too thin. NO is a complete sentence. Find ways and create habits that will keep you whole, sane, and triumphant. You will make mistakes and bad decisions in this life...and that's ok. However, do not continue to make the same bad mistakes because they then become choices. Don't cling to a mistake just because you spent a lot of time making it. There will be times when you don't "feel" like loving yourself, but do it anyway. Declare greatness over yourself every day of your life. There is power in your words. Choose you every single day of the week. Be kind to yourself and give yourself time to evolve and grow. Take moments to evaluate where you are and adjust accordingly. Extend yourself lots of grace and celebrate small wins. When we love something, we take care of it. Your health matters. Your life matters. YOU matter, beautiful black girl.

Reflection

What do you love most about yourself?

_____

_____

_____

_____

_____

_____

_____

_____

_____

_____

_____

_____

_____

_____

_____

_____

_____

_____

Be Yourself

Dear Black Girl,

In a world where people are unsure of who they are, you set the standard. Be bold, and be brave. Be uniquely you. But, in order to do that, you first have to know who you really are. Discovering who you are will be an ongoing process that you will embark on daily, but the core of who you are will be your foundation. Your morals, your values, and your standards will help keep you grounded in this world. However you like your hair, wear it that way and wear it with pride. Do not allow people to tell you who to be if you know that is not authentically who you are. Now, it is important to have positive mentors in your life to help you navigate through the different seasons you will face and to offer you sound advice. However, be careful in that regard. Too many handprints on you will cause you to become little carbon copies of all others. Find your own voice and sing your own song the way you want to sing it. Growth is a decision that you must make. It is ok to quietly step out of a race you don't want to be in, find your own lane, and proceed to win. Some people will not like you and they will live – you will too. Your goal is not to please everyone in this life. And in being you, you don't need the spotlight, just light up the spot! You are allowed to be a work in progress and a masterpiece at the same time. You are enough! Black girl, you are beYOUtiful.

Reflection

What is your best characteristic?

_____

_____

_____

_____

_____

_____

_____

_____

_____

_____

_____

_____

_____

_____

_____

_____

_____

_____

Growth Is A Decision

Dear Black Girl,

Years ago, I heard someone say "growing older is mandatory, but growing up is an option." This statement is so true! Each birthday that you have, you will get older. However, age does not make one an adult. There are many people who are overaged adolescents. Having a purpose and setting attainable goals are sure ways to set you apart from those who are not yet ready to walk in their adulthood. People with a purpose and goals have no time for drama. They invest their energy in things that will add value to their life and the lives of others. Knowing what to respond to is growth. Knowing when to respond is also growth. Understanding that you will always be flawed, but consistently choosing to make a conscious effort to work on those flaws is growth. You see, no one is asking perfection of you. However, most people who are about business do not want unnecessary or invited drama. People will provoke you, this is a fact, but you are not a puppet. The person who "tries" to control you is not your puppet master. Don't allow anyone to think they can just pull your "strings" to make you act out of character or do what they want you to do. No one has control over you and your actions but you. Be accountable for your actions and work to become better. Work to be the BEST YOU every single day. Resolve to grow daily. And, if you should fall, get back up and try again. Failure is not the opposite of success, but rather a part of it.

Reflection

In what areas do you need to grow?

_____

_____

_____

_____

_____

_____

_____

_____

_____

_____

_____

_____

_____

_____

_____

_____

_____

_____

_____

Be Afraid And Do It Anyway

Dear Black Girl,

There will be times in your life when you will be scared to move. Everything will fall right into place, the opportunity will seem too good to be true, and the support you will receive will be overwhelming. Those emotions and feelings will sometimes cause you to be scared and perhaps doubt its authenticity. Those feelings and emotions are ok. A prerequisite for progression is not bravery. Sometimes, you have to do it afraid. Walk out there scared. Do it timidly. When you have really done the work and sowed good seeds, you will reap a harvest. When that time comes for you to reap, be open and ready. Beautiful black girl, being afraid is a natural emotion. It is very normal for you to second guess and doubt your abilities. It is not uncommon for fear to be a powerful force that moves in to try and overtake your bravery. Just remember that you can do it even if you are scared. In this, you will find your true strength, passion and resilience. You will be the epitome of perseverance. Be afraid, but do it anyway, black girl!

Reflection

Think about a time where you have been afraid.

If you haven't experienced that time as of yet, leave the page blank and come back to it when that time comes.

Change The Adjective

Dear Black Girl,

When you google the word "adjective" this comes up: "a word or phrase naming an attribute, added to or grammatically related to a noun to modify or describe it." In short, an adjective describes or modifies a noun. In this life, you, beautiful black girl, will be called many adjectives. Some will be very positive and some not so becoming. Some will describe you and others *may* describe you, but *may* have a negative connotation associated with it. I want to challenge you to change the adjective. You don't have to be what anyone calls you, especially anything that *may* be negative. So, what does that mean? That means you correct people when you hear them call you something that is not necessarily favorable. Let me give you some examples. If someone chooses to call you aggressive, correct them and tell them you are assertive. That simply means you are confident in your strength. If someone chooses to call you bossy, correct them and advise them that you are a leader. That simply means you can be trusted to lead the way. You are not scary, but cautious. You are not difficult, you just tell the truth. You are not awkward; you just ask the tough questions. And if you are ever accused of doing too much, keep taking up space. You don't have to shrink yourself or dim your light to make others comfortable...no ma'am!!

Being different is ok because you attract what is necessary to make you a very rare jewel. Black girl, be YOUnique!

Reflection

What adjective would you like to change?

_____

_____

_____

_____

_____

_____

_____

_____

_____

_____

_____

_____

_____

_____

_____

_____

_____

_____

Check Your Price Tag

Dear Black Girl,

I don't know anyone who doesn't like a deal. When I walk into a store, I am instantly drawn to the clearance racks. I love to see 50-75% off signs in windows. I mean, it does something to my spirit when I can say "look at all I purchased for 'x amount' of dollars." But, beautiful black girl, there are some things that should never be on clearance. Some things are just too valuable to mark down. You see, those things never lose value no matter what. Let's look at a diamond, for instance. Diamonds are known to maintain their value or increase in value over time. Beautiful black girl, you are a diamond. You will never lose your value. Your value will only increase over time. How do you increase your value? I'm glad you asked. The way to increase your value is through obtaining knowledge, reading, experiencing, loving, living, being hopeful, seeing the good in every situation, taking the good with the bad, turning lemons into lemonade, and not allowing anyone or anything to steal your joy. Many more attributes can be added to this list. I also want you to know that diamonds never decrease in value. Your melanin makes you valuable and nothing you can do will decrease your value. The world will make you think that your value will decrease based on some unwise decisions that you may make. Tell them that is invalid information and reject their conclusions about you. Diamonds never lose value over time You will never walk into a jewelry store and find an authentic diamond ring out in the open. You will always find them in a case. Not only will the diamond be in a , case but the case will have a lock on it. If you ever become confused about who you are or how much you are worth, think about the most beautiful diamond you've ever seen. When you think about that diamond, believe that you are even the more valuable. Your presence has power and you are always the priority and not the option. You, black girl, are priceless!

Reflection

What would you add to the list things to make yourself valuable?

_____

_____

_____

_____

_____

_____

_____

_____

_____

_____

_____

_____

Communication Is The Lock; Comprehension Is The Key

Dear Black Girl,

All my life, I have heard communication is key. While I believe communication is vital, I would like to suggest something different. Communication is the lock and comprehension is the key and. Communication is necessary in every aspect of your life. You must learn how to effectively communicate with people on all levels in order to get results. This is something you will not be able to circumvent. However, for you, black girl, you must also learn that comprehension is just as effective as communication. Having a clear understanding of what is being asked of you makes it easier to execute any task. It also leaves little room for gray areas and possible confusion. Practice restating what is asked of you to ensure comprehension. This can be achieved by being an avid reader, increasing your vocabulary and learning the art of speaking correctly. Don't allow anyone to shame you because of how articulate you are. There is no such thing as "talking white." Using the correct English language and vernacular is not associated with an ethnicity, neither is speaking derogatory. Effective communication and comprehension is a choice – one I hope you choose. Beautiful black girl, you are clever, sensible, and perceptive. Once you learn how to communicate and comprehend, you will be an even more powerful force to be reckoned with.

Reflection

Think about a misunderstanding that you may have had in the past. Did ineffective communication play a part in the misunderstanding? What could have been done differently?

_____

_____

_____

_____

_____

_____

_____

_____

_____

_____

_____

_____

_____

_____

_____

_____

_____

_____

Readers Make Leaders

Dear Black Girl,

There is a disturbing quote that I read a few years ago. It said "if you want to hide something from black people, put it in a book." This suggests that black people do not and will not read. My core was disturbed and the English teacher in me was heartbroken. I will not accept this. Hear me and hear me well...readers make leaders. Reading is one of the most liberating things you can do. It is one of the greatest investments that you can make in yourself. You can literally change the trajectory of your life by being informed and by being able to think critically. Reading allows you to define your own success. No one will be able to misconstrue information to you and for you. When you read, a book should be in one hand and a dictionary should be in the other. Being able to read and comprehend several schools of thought provides you with the liberty to say what you mean without saying it mean. Reading unlocks doors, changes lives, and places you in a position to lead. Don't be a part of that quote. Don't let people think that anything can be hidden from you in a book. Prove them wrong! Readers make amazing leaders, and you are destined to lead the way!

Reflection

What is the last book you read? What was it about and how did it help you grow?

If you can't think of one...get to reading!!

_____

_____

_____

_____

_____

_____

_____

_____

_____

_____

_____

_____

_____

_____

_____

_____

_____

_____

_____

_____

Do The Work

Dear Black Girl,

As you grow and evolve into the beautiful creation God has called you to be, don't forget to always do the work to continue to evolve into the best version of yourself. The only person you should ever be in competition with is the old you. Always strive to be the best version of you. This will require work. You see, black girl, no one is going to hand you anything in this life – and if they do, they will want more than you would be willing to pay. So, what do I mean when I say "do the work?" Daily, you should be reading something that will increase your Lexile level and enhance you as a person. Make it a habit to start the day off with a daily declaration that you recite every single day. Allow that declaration to resonate in your spirit throughout your day. Try something new, learn something you didn't know and apply it to your daily life and. Take chances on yourself. And if you think you know it, still be open to learning it another way or enhancing what you already know. Establish a good work ethic in which you can be proud of. Don't ask for handouts. Be willing to put the time, effort, and work into every project you are assigned. Complete tasks with accuracy and fidelity. Allow your work to be a great reflection and representation of who you are. Remain humble and grounded. Get yourself an accountability partner that you trust who can and will hold you responsible and challenge you to be great with no days off. You have places to go, people to impact and a purpose to fulfill. None of that will happen if you do not do the work.

Reflection

What do work can you do to help grow and enhance you.

_____

_____

_____

_____

_____

_____

_____

_____

_____

_____

_____

_____

_____

_____

_____

_____

_____

_____

_____

Enforce Your Boundaries

Dear Black Girl,

Aboundary is defined as "a line that marks the limits of an area." Boundaries are necessary to maintain a healthy and prosperous life. Everyone will have different boundaries for every part of their life. When doing the work to continuously become a better you, you will learn what makes you uncomfortable. When discovering those areas of comfort and discomfort, you begin to understand the line that will mark the limit. When you figure out where that line should be drawn, enforce it. Don't allow anyone to make you compromise your boundaries. Now, evaluations and reevaluations are necessary for continued growth and development. During this time, should you see where a change is necessary that will benefit you and all that you are trying to accomplish, by all means, make the necessary adjustments. But, remember beautiful black girl, these boundaries are yours to set. And when you set them, enforce them at all cost. Setting and enforcing boundaries will help protect your peace and keep you grounded. Should you ever feel like you are off balance and need to readjust, take a look at what you are allowing to happen. If you don't like it, fix it. If you like it, keep doing what you do. But, the key word and person is YOU! You have a right to have boundaries and you absolutely have the right to enforce them at all costs. Don't complain about what you allow. You don't have to set yourself on fire to keep others warm.

Reflection

What boundaries do you have in place?

Are there any more that you need to enforce?

_____

_____

_____

_____

_____

_____

_____

_____

_____

_____

_____

_____

_____

_____

_____

_____

_____

Plan, Pursue, Persevere

Dear Black Girl,

Planning, pursuing and persevering are the three p's that will help you to maintain your focus. In order to be successful, you must have a plan. Now, let me be clear. Just because you make plans doesn't mean everything will go as planned. So, when you plan, keep in mind that you must be flexible and adaptable. Life will happen and that's ok. If plan "A" doesn't work, don't fret; there are 25 more letters in the alphabet. After the plan, you must then begin to prepare and pursue. Now, with that comes discipline and work ethic. You must learn the ends and outs of your craft. You must resolve to take a ride on a highway that may be crowded or even less traveled. Don't allow either to stop your pursuit. Develop great habits along the way that will help you remember your "why." Lastly, beautiful black girl, you must learn the art of perseverance. You must persevere through every challenge that you are faced with. Some will be very difficult – even to the point of making you want to give up and quit. But, listen to me, beautiful black girl, QUITTING IS NOT AN OPTION! Now, should you change your mind, or alter your plans, that is ok...but NEVER give in to defeat or believe that you can't because it gets a little rough. Sometimes, all you need to do is reset, refocus and get it done! Always stay on track and stay focused while remembering those 3 p's.

Reflection

What's your plan for your future?

How will your path get you there?

_____

_____

_____

_____

_____

_____

_____

_____

_____

_____

_____

_____

_____

_____

_____

_____

_____

Progress Vs. Movement

Dear Black Girl,

In these ever-changing times, it is important for you to embrace the pace of your own journey. However, I would like to submit to you that progress is not the same as movement. A rocking chair moves, but remains stationary. Progress is defined as "forward or onward movement towards a destination." Beautiful black girl, make sure that when you are moving, you are progressing. Sometimes, we can have a lot of ideas that we want to accomplish and no plan of action or clear direction to accomplish these goals. It is in that moment that you are "moving" but not progressing. You have to find a way to place yourself into a space that will center and guide your thoughts. You don't want to find yourself doing a lot of things in theory, but in actuality, you've really done nothing at all. The moment you feel like you are a hamster on a wheel spinning and moving, but not progressing, stop and give yourself a break. Give yourself time to rethink and reimagine. No matter what yesterday was like, birds always start the new day with a song. It may just be you need to start the next day and begin a new song with the same tune. So, don't just move, progressively move. And remember, this is your race to run at your own pace. Time goals are necessary to keep you on track; however, allow room for adjustments. You are only human, my dear. You will experience setbacks, but setbacks are usually setups for major comebacks!

Reflection

What are your takeaways?

_____

_____

_____

_____

_____

_____

_____

_____

_____

_____

_____

_____

_____

_____

_____

_____

_____

Thermostat Vs. Thermometer

Dear Black Girl,

As you grow and learn, there will be people who will try to make you lose control of yourself and your emotions. When people know what pushes your buttons, they will always try to get you hot and bothered. Being upset is a normal emotion. Do not allow anyone to make you think otherwise. What I want to propose to you, beautiful black girl, is the control piece. Thermostats can be controlled by an individual whereas thermometers cannot. You can control your own temperature as well as determine how you want to handle a situation. Resist the urge to want to retaliate and spew negativity and harshness towards others. That is very simple to do and does not take much effort. Master the art of self-control. Learn how to be in complete and total control of your feelings, emotions and actions at all times. This is truly a gift. Others will see your willpower and admire you because of it. Constantly remind any and everyone that you are a thermostat and that you control your temperature. One of the beautiful things about black women that I absolutely love is that we have the ability to control any environment, any surrounding and any place that we step foot in. Walk and control fiercely, black beauty! Be a well-poised, well-organized, in control of herself amazing black girl!

Reflection

What do you do when your temperature rises from a situation?

_____

_____

_____

_____

_____

_____

_____

_____

_____

_____

_____

_____

_____

_____

_____

_____

_____

_____

_____

Silence Speaks Volumes

Dear Black Girl,

The world has and continues to paint black girls as loud, boisterous and angry. This stereotype is all too familiar amongst women in the black community. It has been said that we cannot converse with each other without being brash. They use such terms as "ratchet" and "ghetto" to define the black girl and how she responds to situations. I do not accept these adjectives used to describe us. I would like to submit another school of thought. Black girls know when to be silent. She knows that silence is golden. When she does speak, she is able to converse and not crucify. You see, the black girl realizes that people will try to provoke her and try to get her to step out of character. However, she is much smarter than that. She will not fall into the traps and snares of those people and entities to prove their theories to be true. She will surround herself with mentors and friends who will challenge her and hold her accountable for her actions. The black girl is in touch with her feelings and emotions and knows those things that set her off. And, make no mistake about it – every person in the world has at least one thing that will set them off. Some things and people are not worth addressing. If it will cause you to step out of character, be silent. If it has the potential to become drama-filled or messy, remain quiet. If it has the possibility of causing others to view you as angry or not having couth, say nothing. You see, black girl, silence speaks volumes. One thing that I have discovered is irrelevant people HATE remaining irrelevant. Remaining silent keeps those people in the category of irrelevantness. Trust me, this is no easy feat. And I know this can sometimes be a daunting task. But, once you master the art of silence, you will always be triumphant.

Reflection

What was one thing that stood out as you were while reading this chapter?

_____

_____

_____

_____

_____

_____

_____

_____

_____

_____

_____

_____

_____

_____

_____

Use Your Voice

Dear Black Girl,

I have mentioned several times that the black girl knows when to be silent and have even suggested when silence is warranted. However, you do have a voice, and that voice should be used. What you have to say is important and should be heard. Use your voice to speak on those issues that will help build people up and not tear them down. Use your voice to be a calming spirit in the midst chaos. Be a voice of reason to situations and people who need a different perspective. Allow your voice to speak out against bullies and users. Speak up for those who one have no voice or are trying to find their voice. Beautiful black girl, it is important to be open and honest about your feelings so they are not misconstrued. Sometimes, talking through things can be scary and places you in a vulnerable state. This is why it is paramount to be able to articulate yourself in a black and white manner so that your words aren't easily misinterpreted. Use your voice to help and heal. Don't say things out of anger, and correct people in love. There is power in your voice!

Reflection

What is something you need to use your voice to say?

_____

_____

_____

_____

_____

_____

_____

_____

_____

_____

_____

_____

_____

_____

_____

_____

_____

_____

_____

_____

_____

_____

_____

What About Your Friends?

Dear Black Girl,

I am an 80's baby and growing up, I listened to a group by the name of TLC. They made a song very popular titled "What about your friends?" In the song, this girl group asked a series of questions about friends. Listening to the song in my early years, I would just bob my head and sing the lyrics. As I got older, the questions they asked began to resonate in my spirit and made me think of all of the people who I had called my friend. It has been said that young black girls cannot be friends because they despise each other and are jealous of one another. Sometimes, it is engrained in little black girls to be confrontational with their other black sisters and to foster a culture of hate amongst the community of black girls. I want to dispel that today in this moment. We are not people who were created to live in this world alone. True friendships make the world go around and they provide a safe space for comfort and love when the world has tried to beat us up. Friends fight for you, respect you, include you, encourage you, need you, deserve you and stand by you. A true friend will hold you accountable for your actions and help you be better. They say good things behind your back to others and bad things to your face in private. But, in order to have this kind of friend, beautiful black girl, you must first do the work to become this friend. Resist the urge to be catty and confrontational. Every misunderstanding doesn't have to end a friendship or explode into something unnecessary. Learn to communicate in love and express yourself without being offensive. Allow room for growth, error and correction. Learn how to speak the language of friendship with your friends and love them through tough times. Don't be judgmental, but do hold your friends accountable for their actions. And at the end of life's journey, to have a friend with you in the end is a beautiful feeling that can't be replaced with life's finest jewels because true genuine friends are priceless.

Reflection

What qualities do you have inside of you that makes you a great friend?

_____

_____

_____

_____

_____

_____

_____

_____

_____

_____

_____

What Happens When The Friendship Fails?

Dear Black Girl,

It would be irresponsible of me to not address this topic. I believe that friendships are essential to the soul and everyone needs a true friend to help them navigate and journey through this life. But the truth of the matter is, every friendship will not last. Unfortunately, this is a harsh truth I had to face in my adulthood with someone who I believed would always be one of my best friends. I was beyond hurt, but in this hurt, I was able to grow and mature even the more. Beautiful black girl, I want to help you navigate through understanding and getting over a failed friendship should this ever happen to you. Don't ever compromise your integrity or character. If you have been a friend to someone and the friendship ends, that person does not automatically become your enemy. Do NOT share their secrets with anyone. If you were told something in confidence, it should remain there whether you all are still friends or not. You should never degrade them to others or try to blemish their character even if it has been done to you. I know what you are thinking; I hear your thoughts and I know what I am suggesting may seem difficult. But, if you choose to lash out, tell their business, or "defend" their lies, you are no better than them. Remember, silence is also a response. Silence cannot be misquoted. Silence is golden. Allow silence to speak your truth. This does not make you appear weak but strong. It takes strength to handle being lied on and mistreated with grace and class. Do not allow anyone the satisfaction to ever pull you out of character of who you are. Trust me...IT'S HARD!! But, in the end, think of the example you would have given of who you truly are as a person and a friend. Hurt people hurt people. Don't allow your hurt to hurt someone else and don't allow their hurt to damage you. Give yourself time to heal. Don't allow a failed friendship to hinder beautiful friendships that are waiting to happen. Just guard your heart and your mind and be more vigilant. Be aware of signs and address them accordingly. Be sure you are getting what you give. Beautiful black girl, friendships are needed. Girlfriends are sisters we choose for ourselves.

Reflect

What are some ways to handle your emotions if your friendship somehow fails?

_____

_____

_____

_____

_____

_____

Get You A Mentor

Dear Black Girl,

Google defines mentor as "an experienced or trusted advisor." It is paramount that you as a black girl connect with someone who can serve as a mentor. When I was 20 years old, I met a lady while I was in college who, unbeknownst to me, would serve as my lifelong mentor. I entered into the Miss Albany State University pageant and she was the pageant director. During our practices, she would watch me, talk to me, and got to know me as a person. I will never know why we connected the way we did, but I will always be grateful for this connection. She is educated, bright, very witty, extremely funny and brilliant. She can do anything – like ANYTHING. She is the true definition of a "girl boss" and "black girl magic." Over time, she helped me grow by telling me hard truths about myself. I was able to recognize that it was out of love. She encouraged me to be the best version of myself while always being the best version of herself. I watched her. I listened to her. I grew from her and as a result, we have a bond that has lasted for almost 20 years. She is graceful and wise. She is pure and genuine. She is strong and meek. Every place I wanted to go, she had already been. She provided me with the blueprint to those places but still encouraged me to create my own path. She spoke to me with love, even when she chastened me. Every word, every action, every deed was received with an open heart and mind. I made the decision to use all of these tools to help me grow and evolve into who I know I am called to be. She kept her hands on me, never letting me fall; and for that, I am grateful. Beautiful black girl, a large part of who I have become as an adult is because of the connection I made with her. Get yourself someone who can speak life in you. Find you a person who sees potential in you and helps you tap into it. And lastly, connect with a soul who will love you back to life even when you feel like you don't have any life left.

Reflection

Who is a black woman that inspires you?

How does she enhance you?

_____

_____

_____

_____

_____

_____

_____

_____

_____

_____

_____

_____

Enemy Vs. Inner Me

Dear Black Girl,

An enemy is "a person who is actively opposed or hostile to someone or something." Usually, we see enemies as other people who don't want to see us succeed or who intentionally try to place barriers in our way to make it difficult or impossible for us to win. Allow me to caution you, beautiful black girl, to not allow your enemy to be your inner me. It is important to take necessary steps to build up your self-esteem. Practice affirming you to yourself so that when someone shows up to try to tell you otherwise, you already know who you are. You are bold, strong, wise, patient, beautiful and creative. You will not always have it together and that is ok. Allow yourself time and space for growth. Learn from the mistakes and mishaps of others. You are not an option. Know your own truth so you can spot the error. Make it a habit to put you first. And when you are not really "feeling like it," take a moment to gather yourself. Do whatever you need to do to block out the noise and refocus. There will be people in this life that will try to tear your down and rip you apart. Don't ever join in with them and help them. Recognize that you are not your enemy. Protect your peace, protect your mind, and guard your heart.

Reflection

What is inside of you that you need to address that could hinder your success?

_____

_____

_____

_____

_____

_____

_____

_____

_____

_____

_____

_____

_____

_____

_____

_____

_____

_____

_____

_____

_____

_____

You Either Win Or You Learn

Dear Black Girl,

Every now and then, when you put your mind to something and execute it, you will not always be successful the first time. Some people would call that a failure. I would like to submit another school of thought. You do not lose, you either win or you learn. F.A.I.L only means (F)irst (A)ttempt (I)n (L)earning. If whatever you attempt does not work out the first time, try it again. The second time, you are executing with experience. When things do not go as planned, that is ok. Learn to be flexible and adjust. Be humble and not prideful. Sometimes, it may be that something could have been done better. Other times, it might be something like timing or lack of experience. Now, let us discuss what a win really is. The definition of win according to google is to "be successful or victorious in (a contest or conflict)." But, beautiful black girl, being victorious can look a little different. No's are simply "not yets." In your "not yet" moments, you gain experience, new perspectives, and knowledge. Winning is not always about being victorious, but rather learning. Focusing on (W)hat's (I)mportant (N)ow is a sure way to be a winner. Sometimes, all you need is a second chance because you were not ready for the first one.

What lessons have you learned over the last six months?

How will you turn these lessons into wins?

_____

_____

_____

_____

_____

_____

_____

_____

_____

_____

_____

_____

_____

_____

_____

_____

_____

_____

_____

_____

_____

Examples Of Black Girl Magic

Listed below are names of phenomenal women who have changed and enhanced many lives of all races of people. On the left is their name – on the right are some things that makes them amazing. Several columns are available for you to add to this list. Use this as encouragement and motivation to work daily to be your best self. And, don't forget to add your name to the list, beautiful black girl. You are phenomenal, too!

Michelle Obama	First African American woman to be the First Lady Of The United States (FLOTUS)
Kamala Harris	First African American woman to be the Vice President of the United States of America. HBCU graduate
Stacey Abrams	African American politician who used defeat to change the trajectory of Georgia in the 2020 presidential election. HBCU graduate
Keisha Lance Bottoms	African American politician and lawyer who is the Mayor of Atlanta, Ga. HBCU graduate
Kimberly Lowe Abad	Author, Business Owner, Life Coach, Educator HBCU graduate

Black Girl Daily Declaration

I am bold, confident and proud

My worth is priceless

My passion is unmatched

I love myself

Hard work defines me

Leadership describes me

I am confident, not cocky

Aware, not arrogant

A higher power guides me

I believe in me, my ability

I will do the work, the hard work

I will be all that I am designed to be

Because greatness will always be my portion

Speak greatness over yourself every single day! Feel free to add to or enhance this declaration. Words are powerful! Life and death are in the power of the tongue. Speak life!!

Made in the USA
Middletown, DE
08 November 2021